The Book of Muses

poems by

Judith Sornberger

Finishing Line Press
Georgetown, Kentucky

The Book of Muses

Copyright © 2023 by Judith Sornberger
ISBN 979-8-88838-257-8 First Edition
All rights reserved under International and Pan-American Copyright Conventions. No part of this book may be reproduced in any manner whatsoever without written permission from the publisher, except in the case of brief quotations embodied in critical articles and reviews.

ACKNOWLEDGMENTS

The author thanks the initial publishers of the following poems that were published under slightly different titles:

"The Muse as Grosbeak" and "Crossroads" in *The Grotto Network*
"The Muse, Weaving" in *Ruminate*
"The Muse, as Garter Snake, Drops You a Line" in *Presence: A Journal of Catholic Poetry*
"The Muse, as Nurse Log, Lets Hersaelf Go" in *Chautauqua*
"The Muse Pedals Up Behind You" in *Northern Appalachian Review*
"Like the Moon, the Muse Pulls at You" in *The Windhover*

Publisher: Leah Huete de Maines
Editor: Christen Kincaid
Cover Art: Sarah Kiser
Author Photo: Karl Schneider
Cover Design: Elizabeth Maines McCleavy

Order online: www.finishinglinepress.com
also available on amazon.com

Author inquiries and mail orders:
Finishing Line Press
PO Box 1626
Georgetown, Kentucky 40324
USA

Table of Contents

The Muse as Source 1

Crossroads 2

The Muse Speaks of Creation 3

Early Morning, the Muse Is at Your Window 4

The Muse as Painted Turtle 5

The Muse Pedals Up Behind You 6

The Muse Comes in Summer 8

The Muse as Red-breasted Grosbeak 9

Evil Muse Says 10

The Muse as Black Bear 11

The Muse Is a Witch 12

Like the Moon, the Muse Pulls at You 14

Mermaid Muse 15

The Muse, as Garter Snake, Drops You a Line 16

The Muse as Goldfinch 17

The Muse Recommends the *Via Negativa* 18

The Muse, as Nurse Log, Lets Herself Go 19

The Muse, Weaving 20

To Karl Schneider whose love, kindness, and deep wisdom about the natural world always inspire me

The Muse as Source

The muse is a small dark pond,
the ink-black base
of everything
alive on this binding
from a 16th century
collection of Persian poetry
reproduced on the journal
I write in.

It's night, and a slender
deer tiptoes near
to sip from her perimeter,
while another circles
itself into sleep beneath
cinnabar-blossomed limbs
whose roots lose
themselves in her loam.

Birds with long, elaborate
tails return to roost
in the loose weave
of swaying branches.
Below them, a lone
brown duck with onyx
head and orange beak
floats on her surface.

Darkness is so deep,
water, land and air
seep into one another,
entering the common
dream of our creation.

Crossroads

The Muse is the doe
in the road you miss
hitting, the one crossing
on cautious hooves,
sniffing the air
for your secrets.
On the other side,
she turns back, gazing
with a curious gleam
as if asking what you
mean if not danger.
Now she's leaping
off with a flick
of white tail you take
as invitation.
You may follow
her through mist
between the trees,
beside the marsh or stream,
through the bright
and dull seasons of wings.
All she asks is that
you forget your car,
your destination, and every
map you've ever believed in.

The Muse Speaks of Creation

Occasionally, we stretch time
so thin it can forget to fly,
and morphs into a landscape
of far stars, a map of boundless
hope or endless sighs.

Occasionally, we sketch rhyme
into the days where we reside—
echoes of congruence, reminders
of how other creatures are our teachers,
of how *to listen* can create *to glisten*.

Occasionally, we catch the sublime
out of the corner of an eye, turn
to watch, forgetting, for an instant,
we've latched ourselves to
some presumably essential task.

Occasionally, we patch a line
onto a poem the way a skater
adds an extra leap over
the ice, because the music
told her it was right.

Occasionally, we etch a design
that may have climbed out
of the Divine and wedged itself
into some yet uncluttered
edge of the heart's mind, waiting
till we reached for it, in time.

Early Morning, the Muse Is at Your Window
after the oil painting Karen's House *by H.M. Levan*

She pours herself
    into your room
        in a misty
           gown of sunlight—
    an organza river
        glazing
        the floorboards—
           a beckoning
        glisten—
          offering an
            aisle of wonder.

Don't even
glance at the
grandfather
clock in the
corner—its
towering
insistence on
hours and
minutes. Do
not listen for
its ticking.

        The Muse has turned
      the clock's moon face
        to a dazed blur—
          nearly erased its hands,
            unwinding
              time.
          Now
                wade
            into the glimmer
            and step through her.

The Muse as Painted Turtle

When she climbs the steep bank
from the marsh, digging claws
into the mud, hoisting her shell,
she has only one intention—
to reach the top, find a dry, flat space,
and burrow deep to lay her eggs.
She won't know if they'll be safe
from hungry skunks, foxes, or raccoons,
if they'll be allowed to incubate
for sixty days. Or whether a single
hatchling will make it to the water
chased by beaks and bills and teeth.

So is it really so hard, she asks,
for you to claw past obstacles—
fear and lists and laziness—
between you and your desk, to sit
patiently until something comes?
So what if you don't know
whether an image, memory or idea
will survive the page.
Your job is just to lay your eggs—to wait
and watch, to greet what emerges.

The Muse Pedals Up Behind You

Silver bangles ringing at her wrists
like the bell on your first bike.
She stops to pet your pup, says you look
familiar, asks how many snappers
you've spotted laying eggs along the path.
Five, you say. She's seen seven.
You add an eagle; she's seen two.

Once you've told your bike path tales,
you admire her jewelry—bracelets studded
with berry-bright gems; a turquoise pendant,
and beaded earrings so long they brush
her tan shoulders. When she grins
and gives her head a shake to twirl them,
her pewter curls spring to life.

They have stories, you know,
she says in a conspiratorial tone—
Where you found them, who gave them
to you, who wore them before you.
You want to show her your rings—
your father's gold pinky with its diamond
that your mother kept until she died.

And the forget-me-not blue oval—
a calm pond set in silver—
your husband gave you
the birthday before his death.
Some say larimar is a healing stone.

And the ring slipped on your finger
years later by your lover—an aquamarine
floating on white-gold waves. Some say
these sea-blue stones washed up from
the spilled treasure chests of Sirens.

You want to tell their stories,
but the Muse is wheeling off,
tires spinning like old movie reels,
like stories with no endings.
Over her shoulder she calls:
Keep counting those turtles!

The Muse Comes in Summer

Sings jump rope rhymes into your sleep—
My mama, your mama live across the street . . . .
Wakes you up early to look for lucky
beans hidden in leathery pods under locust trees.
She dares you to swing on a rope
from the highest pine in the neighborhood,
to let go and jump over the terrace
like a paratrooper—the only girl
in the Crown Point Avenue Army.
When you yearn for a skateboard,
she inspires you take apart a roller skate
and nail the parts to the front and back
of a two by four left over when your dad
finished the basement. The Muse calls
you to round up the kids on the block
and put on a play about dolls
who come alive at midnight,
as you've always suspected they do.
The garage for your stage, its door pulled
up and down as a curtain, folding chairs
on the driveway for your audience.
After supper, the Muse calls down the dark,
climbs beside you in the hammock, and listens
to lullabies you sing to the stars.

The Muse as Rose-breasted Grosbeak

The Muse is a bird you lure
with the seed of attention.
You invite, you wait, you work.
She may show up, or not.
She doesn't belong to you
or care if you catch
sight of Her. She may
even appear as a male—
black and white wings
flashing toward your feeder,
the bird perching there,
taking his time and finally
turning to reveal the shock
of scarlet bright as a gunshot
wound against the white chest.

Not all your wounds are visible.
Surely not the one beating
in your heart. The Muse calls
it to the surface, calls you
to wear it like a ruby pendant
searing your skin until pain turns
slowly into beauty as you write it.
Until the grosbeak vanishes
into the trees, warbling
for its mate, and you call
back with this poem.

Evil Muse Says

Go ahead!
Paint the portrait
of the friend who
fucked you over.
Broaden that sanctimonious
smile that whispered your
confessions in other ears.
Stain the teeth darker
yellow. Better yet, blur
her eyes with sorrow.
Paint her twenty years
from now—alive
or in her coffin.
Go on!
Thin her hair,
Tint it ash gray.
Deepen those ugly
lines between nose
and upper lip—
an affliction
you both share.
Try not to feel
compassion for
the woman
you've created.

The Muse as Black Bear

Some days the Muse
is a bear perched like Buddha
on the wooded hill
behind your house.
She peers at you
through silver-green
juniper—eyes sad
and wise as a sage.

You yearn to step into
the deep nap of her fur,
to be folded into her embrace.
But the Muse is no teddy bear.

She's not here
to sing you lullabies.
Or to press her long cinnamon
snout into your neck,
pouring all the rhythms
of the wild into your ear.

Understand, there is danger,
but don't back away or startle.
Everything you need
dwells in her close-set eyes.
Hold still and hold her gaze
as long as she'll allow it,
as long as you dare.

The Muse Is a Witch

living deep in the woods—
the magic pulsing
of its green heart.
She's the queen
of transformation,
and you are her subject,
her servant, her student.

To serve her, rise
at first birdcall,
fill an offering basket
with hen-of-the-woods
mushrooms, and follow
fallen petals and tracks
of wild turkeys to the oak
with furrows so deep
and wide, they're footholds.

Climb to her stick-built cabin
resting like a nest
in the tree's mighty limbs
and hope for welcome.
You never know
if she'll be home.
In a dark mood, she'll go
off for hours, gathering
ferns, mosses and feathers
for a new dress; hibiscus,
lemon balm and spearmint
for a tincture to help her
feel better. No matter.

Everything here speaks
of her. Everything's
an invitation to create
something from what
looks like nothing.

Wipe the mist from the mirror
behind her bubbling
cauldron, and memories
appear, ones that you'd
forgotten, that beg
to go on living.

Even the corner spider web
inspires you to swirl
something gorgeous from
the dormancy inside you.
Sit down in her overstuffed
armchair, let her ginger tabby
turn circles in your lap,
spinning a spell of purring
and surrender to enchantment.

Like the Moon, the Muse Pulls at You
From the painting Song of the Rio Grande *by Meinrad Craighead*

Beneath the wild bouquet of gray braids
springing from her skull, the Muse's
weeping is an invocation she plays
on a cello strung with the hair
of the dead, their voices a river-
weave of *diminuendo* and *crescendo*,
pulling an ancient keening from the wolf
beside her, calling tears to fill the deep
arroyos in your face, your heart, your soul.

Oh yes, she dares you to use the word
soul, well knowing poets are admonished
not to. She sets it loose in you—*soul*—
the O-O-O-O coursing through
your body like the violet-tinged river—
singing over her naked feet. O-O-O-O—
the white cry of the moon rising
behind her. O-O-O-O howling from
your riverbed of sorrows.

Mermaid Muse

She watches you swim your dutiful laps
    from her perch at the pool's edge.
        Unruly auburn waves veil her breasts,
            and her tail is an emerald shimmer—
                the mermaid you imagined
      you were as a girl, undulating
  like a dolphin or otter
in the chlorine-scented sea
    of the Keystone Pool in Omaha, Nebraska.
          The Muse croons a meterless tune
      in a voice like the underwater hum
    when you stayed down at the bottom
    as long as you could, feet
        and bony knees pressed into a tail, propelling
            you to the surface to gulp air—
        long hair streaming over your back
      and narrow shoulders
like seaweed, diamond
    droplets clinging to the
            down on your arms.

Learning the elements in school, you figured you were born
in the wrong one—your body so awkward on the playground,
so lithe and strong in water. It made no sense The Little Mermaid
left that buoyancy for some dumb boy. *And gave up her voice,*
    the Muse reminds you, coaxing you out of your lane

                                        to dip
                        and glide,
            to bounce
and splash
                        and swirl,

to give up nothing of the girl
    who follows you still—sun shadow,
        glittering ripple—your guide
to leaping between worlds.

The Muse, as Garter Snake, Drops You a Line,

leaves her discarded skin beside your door—
long tunnel of parchment you could read
as a sinuous pause in a melodic line—
a memory you follow, flute to lips,
and breathe into new life.

You could read it as a line, in a sketch
of ink and pen, becoming a small boat
nearly hidden in the reeds—so far away
you can't see where the fisherman's
line sinks into the stream. Yet you feel
the gentle tug, the nibble in the darkness
of something wanting to be born,
and your skin prickles like the water's
as you pull sun-spangled scales
and splashing anguish to the surface.

You could read it as a seam you might stitch
between countries of pigments and patterns,
between centuries and seasons,
between this life and the next one.
A seam to reunite, in new designs,
small pieces of the world as it unravels.

The Muse as Goldfinch

Even the Muse
sometimes loses
most of her color.
Yet faithful
as a gray-
robed monk
at his prayers,
she keeps appearing
at the feeder
over that long winter
until one day—
as if by grace
or patience—
her feathers begin
to recall—
as will yours
she seems to promise—
all their gold,
their true
illumination.

The Muse Recommends the *Via Negativa*

The Muse takes you sailing
with no destination in sight
unless the sun crowning
crimson on the horizon
like the birth of time
could be called one.

As though the endless rocking
of the waves below you
were music you could swallow,
its salt spray tickling
the back of your throat.

As though leaving the shore
of the familiar with no baggage,
phone or map were a necessary
voyage to nowhere in particular.

As though the mystery of the depths
might flash into the light,
revealing itself as the reason
God gave you eyes.

As though the sky's hung out
her every-changing sheets of sapphire,
silver-blue, opalescent pink, pulling
them aside like translucent curtains
you pass through, light dripping
on your shoulders, absorbing you
in mists where you can be no one.

The Muse, as Nurse Log, Lets Herself Go
from the oil painting Spring Ramps and Hepatica *by H.M. Levan*

Once home to the voices of orioles
and thrushes, the Muse's green crown
is long gone, as she lays herself
down on the forest floor.
Though roots no longer feed her,
she offers sustenance to all
that creep over or sleep beneath her.

As her skin decays, a new velvet one
covers her in a full palette of green—
emerald, chartreuse, olive—holding
moisture for jade ferns springing from her,
while, nearby, translucent tongues
of celadon sing her goodness.

She allows her heartwood
to be humbled into humus,
opening a cave spilling petite
white blossoms like the first stars
into the woods' dark cosmos.

She invites you to lie down
beside her, to inhale the sweet
scent of rot as she feeds microbes
and wakes seedlings, calling forth
what waits for life within you.

The Muse, Weaving
> —*from the mural* Weaving *by Diego Rivera*

I want to believe nothing is lost—

    not a leaf or syllable,

not a snip of thread or needle,

        that the cobalt blue cabinet

    holds everything that's passed

      beyond our vision,

that the kneeling woman before it

      weaves the white hair of the dead,

  sinews of April skies,

        ebony of fallen feathers

and red streamers of sunsets

        into a fresh pattern

  ancient as the mind of God.

        I want to see the lapis waves

of her skirt as the sea

    we all began in,

  to believe the braid down her back

holds codes for streams and paths,

      languages and equations,

    that the fabric rolled in her lap
        is the map of a new beginning.

With Thanks

First, a big thank you to Marjorie Saiser. Reading her wonderful poem "The Muse is a Little Girl" (*The Track the Whales Make*) inspired the beginnings of this collection.

Big love and thanks to Alison Townsend, writing partner and *anam cara*, whose poetry and prose is an ongoing source of inspiration, and whose close readings of these poems has vastly improved them.

Many thanks and love to Lilace Mellin Guignard for her brilliant comments on this manuscript and for always helping me to find new possibilities in my writing. Thanks for finding inspiring places for us to go write together.

Deepest gratitude to my friend Karen Meyers, who frequently gets me out for walks along Pine Creek.

For friendship, laughter, and her beautiful poems, gratitude to Marjorie Maddox.

Judith Sornberger's full-length poetry collections are: *Angel Chimes: Poems of Advent and Christmas* (Shanti Arts, 2020), *I Call to You from Time* (Wipf & Stock, 2019), *Practicing the World* (CavanKerry, 2018) and *Open Heart* (Calyx Books). Her prose memoir The Accidental Pilgrim: Finding God and His Mother in Tuscany is from Shanti Arts. She is professor emerita of Mansfield University where she taught English and Women's Studies. She lives on the side of a mountain outside Wellsboro, PA, where the Muse visits nearly every day. www.judithsornberger.net.

www.ingramcontent.com/pod-product-compliance
Lightning Source LLC
Chambersburg PA
CBHW022129090426
42743CB00008B/1066